50 Cooking with Kids: Easy Recipes for Home

By: Kelly Johnson

Table of Contents

- Peanut Butter and Banana Roll-Ups
- Mini Fruit Pizzas
- Veggie Quesadillas
- Ants on a Log (celery with peanut butter and raisins)
- Easy Homemade Pizza
- Rainbow Fruit Kabobs
- Cheese and Veggie Pita Pockets
- Apple Sandwiches with Granola and Peanut Butter
- DIY Trail Mix
- Yogurt Parfait Bar
- Homemade Applesauce
- Veggie and Cheese Omelette
- Banana Sushi (banana rolled in peanut butter and cereal)
- Mini Meatball Subs
- Cheesy Broccoli Bites
- English Muffin Pizzas
- Turkey and Cheese Roll-Ups
- No-Bake Energy Bites
- Fruit and Cheese Skewers
- Pancake Dippers with Fruit
- Rice Cake Toppings Bar
- Taco Cups
- Mini Bagel Pizzas
- Apple Nachos (sliced apples topped with peanut butter and granola)
- Veggie and Hummus Wraps
- DIY Smoothie Bowls
- Grilled Cheese Roll-Ups
- Fruit and Yogurt Popsicles
- Baked Zucchini Fries
- DIY Sushi Rolls (using cucumber, avocado, and cream cheese)
- Turkey and Veggie Pinwheels
- Baked Chicken Tenders
- Cheese and Crackers Snack Platter
- Veggie Chips (baked slices of sweet potato, zucchini, or carrot)
- Mini Corn Dog Muffins

- Peanut Butter and Jelly Sushi Rolls
- Carrot and Hummus Snack Packs
- Baked Apple Chips
- Mini Quiches
- DIY Fruit Leather
- Caprese Skewers (tomato, mozzarella, and basil)
- Turkey and Veggie Stir-Fry
- Veggie Pita Pizzas
- Banana Oatmeal Cookies
- Mini Tacos
- Ham and Cheese Pinwheels
- Sweet Potato Toast with Toppings
- Cucumber Sandwiches
- DIY Fruit Cups
- Cheesy Cauliflower Bites

Peanut Butter and Banana Roll-Ups

Ingredients:

- 1 medium banana
- 2 tablespoons peanut butter (or any nut or seed butter of your choice)
- 1 large whole wheat or flour tortilla

Instructions:

1. Peel the banana and place it on a cutting board. Use a butter knife to spread the peanut butter evenly over the entire surface of the banana.
2. Place the tortilla on a clean surface. Carefully place the peanut butter-covered banana on one end of the tortilla.
3. Gently roll the tortilla around the banana, starting from the end closest to the banana and rolling towards the other end. Make sure the banana is securely wrapped in the tortilla.
4. If desired, you can slice the rolled-up banana into smaller pieces to make it easier to eat, or you can leave it whole for a bigger snack.
5. Serve immediately and enjoy your Peanut Butter and Banana Roll-Ups!

Feel free to get creative with this recipe by adding additional ingredients like honey, cinnamon, or sliced strawberries before rolling up the tortilla. It's a versatile and customizable snack that kids will love making and eating!

Mini Fruit Pizzas

Ingredients:

- 1 package of pre-made sugar cookie dough (or homemade sugar cookie dough)
- 1 cup of cream cheese, softened
- 1/4 cup of powdered sugar
- 1 teaspoon of vanilla extract
- Assorted fruits (such as strawberries, kiwi, blueberries, raspberries, pineapple, etc.), washed, peeled, and sliced
- Optional: honey or fruit preserves for drizzling

Instructions:

1. Preheat your oven according to the instructions on the sugar cookie dough package.
2. Roll out the sugar cookie dough on a floured surface to about 1/4 inch thickness. Use a cookie cutter or a small cup to cut out small circles from the dough.
3. Place the cookie dough circles on a baking sheet lined with parchment paper, leaving some space between each one.
4. Bake the cookie dough circles according to the package instructions, until they are golden brown and cooked through. Remove from the oven and let them cool completely.
5. In a mixing bowl, combine the softened cream cheese, powdered sugar, and vanilla extract. Mix until smooth and creamy.
6. Once the cookie dough circles have cooled, spread a layer of the cream cheese mixture on top of each one.
7. Arrange the sliced fruits on top of the cream cheese mixture, creating colorful and decorative patterns.
8. If desired, drizzle a little honey or fruit preserves over the top of the fruit for added sweetness.
9. Serve the Mini Fruit Pizzas immediately, or store them in the refrigerator until ready to serve. Enjoy!

These Mini Fruit Pizzas are not only delicious but also fun to make. Kids can get creative with their fruit toppings, making each pizza unique and colorful. It's a perfect treat for parties, snack time, or dessert!

Veggie Quesadillas

Ingredients:

- 4 large flour tortillas
- 1 cup shredded cheese (cheddar, Monterey Jack, or a Mexican blend)
- 1 bell pepper, thinly sliced
- 1 small onion, thinly sliced
- 1 cup sliced mushrooms
- 1 cup baby spinach leaves
- 1 tablespoon olive oil
- Salt and pepper to taste
- Optional toppings: salsa, guacamole, sour cream

Instructions:

1. Heat the olive oil in a large skillet over medium heat. Add the sliced bell pepper, onion, and mushrooms. Season with salt and pepper to taste. Cook for 5-7 minutes, or until the vegetables are tender.
2. Remove the vegetables from the skillet and set aside. Wipe the skillet clean with a paper towel.
3. Place one tortilla in the skillet over medium heat. Sprinkle a quarter of the shredded cheese evenly over half of the tortilla.
4. Add a quarter of the cooked vegetables and a handful of baby spinach leaves on top of the cheese.
5. Fold the tortilla in half to cover the filling, creating a half-moon shape. Press down gently with a spatula.
6. Cook the quesadilla for 2-3 minutes on each side, or until the tortilla is golden brown and the cheese is melted.
7. Remove the quesadilla from the skillet and place it on a cutting board. Let it cool for a minute before slicing it into wedges.
8. Repeat the process with the remaining tortillas and filling ingredients.
9. Serve the veggie quesadillas hot with optional toppings such as salsa, guacamole, or sour cream.

These veggie quesadillas are packed with flavor and nutrients, making them a great option for a quick and healthy meal. Plus, they're easy enough for kids to help assemble, making them a fun cooking project for the whole family!

Ants on a Log (celery with peanut butter and raisins)

Ingredients:

- Celery stalks, washed and trimmed
- Peanut butter (or any nut or seed butter of your choice)
- Raisins

Instructions:

1. Cut the celery stalks into manageable lengths, typically about 3 to 4 inches long.
2. Spread peanut butter evenly into the hollowed-out part of each celery stalk. You can use a butter knife or a small spoon to do this.
3. Place raisins on top of the peanut butter-filled celery stalks. These will resemble the "ants" on the log.
4. Arrange the Ants on a Log on a serving plate or tray.
5. Serve and enjoy!

This snack is not only tasty but also provides a good balance of protein, healthy fats, and fiber. It's a great option for a quick snack or a fun addition to a children's party or gathering. Feel free to get creative by adding other toppings like chocolate chips, shredded coconut, or dried cranberries.

Easy Homemade Pizza

Ingredients:

- 1 pre-made pizza crust (store-bought or homemade)
- 1/2 cup pizza sauce
- 1 to 1 1/2 cups shredded mozzarella cheese
- Your choice of toppings (such as sliced pepperoni, diced bell peppers, sliced onions, sliced mushrooms, olives, etc.)

Instructions:

1. Preheat your oven according to the instructions on the pizza crust package or your homemade crust recipe.
2. Place the pizza crust on a pizza pan or baking sheet lined with parchment paper.
3. Spread the pizza sauce evenly over the surface of the pizza crust, leaving a small border around the edges.
4. Sprinkle the shredded mozzarella cheese evenly over the sauce-covered crust.
5. Add your desired toppings on top of the cheese. Get creative and customize your pizza with your favorite ingredients!
6. Once you've added all your toppings, place the pizza in the preheated oven.
7. Bake the pizza according to the instructions on the pizza crust package or your homemade crust recipe, typically for 10-15 minutes or until the crust is golden brown and the cheese is bubbly and melted.
8. Remove the pizza from the oven and let it cool for a few minutes before slicing.
9. Slice the pizza into wedges or squares and serve hot.

Enjoy your delicious homemade pizza! You can experiment with different crusts, sauces, cheeses, and toppings to create endless flavor combinations. It's a great way to involve kids in the kitchen and let them get creative with their food.

Rainbow Fruit Kabobs

Ingredients:

- Assorted fruits in various colors (such as strawberries, pineapple chunks, oranges, kiwi slices, blueberries, grapes, and raspberries)
- Wooden skewers

Instructions:

1. Wash and prepare all the fruits. If necessary, slice larger fruits like strawberries, oranges, and kiwi into bite-sized pieces.
2. Assemble the fruit kabobs by threading the prepared fruits onto the wooden skewers in a rainbow pattern, alternating colors as you go. For example, start with red fruits (like strawberries), followed by orange fruits (like oranges), then yellow fruits (like pineapple), green fruits (like kiwi), blue and purple fruits (like blueberries and grapes), and finally, finish with red or pink fruits (like raspberries or more strawberries).
3. Continue threading the fruits onto the skewers until you reach the desired length, leaving some space at the bottom of the skewer for easy handling.
4. Repeat the process with the remaining skewers until you have made enough rainbow fruit kabobs for serving.
5. Arrange the fruit kabobs on a serving platter or tray, making sure to display their vibrant colors.
6. Serve the rainbow fruit kabobs immediately as a healthy and colorful snack or dessert option for parties, gatherings, or simply as a fun treat.

These Rainbow Fruit Kabobs are not only delicious and nutritious but also visually stunning, making them a hit with both kids and adults alike. Feel free to customize the fruit selection based on personal preferences or seasonal availability. Enjoy the burst of colors and flavors with every bite!

Cheese and Veggie Pita Pockets

Ingredients:

- Whole wheat pita bread
- Cheese slices or shredded cheese (cheddar, mozzarella, or your favorite cheese)
- Assorted veggies (such as sliced cucumber, bell peppers, tomatoes, lettuce, shredded carrots, or any other veggies you like)
- Hummus or Greek yogurt (optional, for spreading)

Instructions:

1. Cut the whole wheat pita bread in half to create pockets. If the pockets are too thick, you can gently separate the two layers to create more room for filling.
2. If using cheese slices, place them inside the pita pockets. If using shredded cheese, sprinkle it inside the pockets.
3. Add your choice of assorted veggies into the pita pockets. Get creative and layer them according to your preference. You can mix and match different veggies for added flavor and texture.
4. If desired, spread a layer of hummus or Greek yogurt inside the pita pockets before adding the veggies. This will add extra creaminess and flavor to the filling.
5. Once the pita pockets are filled with cheese and veggies, gently press down on them to pack the filling tightly.
6. Serve the cheese and veggie pita pockets immediately, or wrap them in foil or parchment paper for an on-the-go meal or snack option.

These Cheese and Veggie Pita Pockets are versatile and customizable, making them a great option for lunch, dinner, or even a quick snack. You can also experiment with different cheese and veggie combinations to suit your taste preferences. Enjoy the delicious and wholesome flavors in every bite!

Apple Sandwiches with Granola and Peanut Butter

Ingredients:

- 1 large apple (any variety you prefer)
- Peanut butter (or any nut or seed butter of your choice)
- Granola (homemade or store-bought)

Instructions:

1. Wash the apple thoroughly and slice it horizontally into thick slices, about 1/4 to 1/2 inch thick. You can remove the core and seeds if desired, or leave them intact for added crunch.
2. Spread peanut butter evenly on one side of each apple slice. You can use a butter knife or a small spoon to do this.
3. Sprinkle granola generously over the peanut butter on one of the apple slices. Make sure to cover the entire surface.
4. Place the other apple slice on top of the granola-covered slice, creating a sandwich.
5. Press down gently to secure the sandwich together and ensure that the peanut butter sticks to the granola.
6. Repeat the process to make more apple sandwiches with the remaining apple slices.
7. Serve the apple sandwiches immediately, or wrap them in plastic wrap or parchment paper for an on-the-go snack.

These apple sandwiches with granola and peanut butter are not only delicious but also packed with fiber, protein, and healthy fats, making them a satisfying and energizing snack option. They're perfect for a quick breakfast, midday snack, or even a light lunch. Enjoy the crunchy, sweet, and creamy combination with every bite!

DIY Trail Mix

Ingredients:

- Nuts (such as almonds, cashews, peanuts, walnuts, pecans, or mixed nuts)
- Seeds (such as pumpkin seeds, sunflower seeds, or sesame seeds)
- Dried fruits (such as raisins, cranberries, apricots, cherries, mango, pineapple, or apple)
- Optional additions (such as dark chocolate chips, coconut flakes, pretzel pieces, cereal, popcorn, or yogurt-covered raisins)

Instructions:

1. Start by selecting your desired nuts, seeds, and dried fruits. You can choose a variety of options or focus on a few favorites.
2. Measure out the desired quantities of each ingredient and place them in a large mixing bowl.
3. Mix the nuts, seeds, and dried fruits together until evenly distributed.
4. If adding any optional additions like chocolate chips or coconut flakes, gently fold them into the mixture.
5. Once all the ingredients are combined, transfer the trail mix to an airtight container or individual snack bags for storage.
6. Enjoy your DIY trail mix as a convenient and nutritious snack on the go, or pack it for hiking, camping, road trips, or school and work lunches.

Trail mix is highly versatile, so feel free to experiment with different ingredient combinations and ratios to find your perfect mix. You can also adjust the sweetness and saltiness levels to suit your taste preferences. Have fun creating and snacking on your personalized trail mix!

Yogurt Parfait Bar

Ingredients and Supplies:

- Plain or flavored yogurt (Greek yogurt or regular yogurt)
- Assorted toppings (such as granola, fresh fruits, dried fruits, nuts, seeds, honey, maple syrup, chocolate chips, coconut flakes, etc.)
- Serving bowls or cups
- Spoons
- Napkins

Instructions:

1. Prepare the yogurt: Arrange bowls or containers of plain and flavored yogurt on a table or countertop. You can offer different yogurt options to accommodate various taste preferences.
2. Set out the toppings: Arrange a variety of toppings in separate bowls or containers. Some popular options include granola, sliced strawberries, blueberries, raspberries, sliced bananas, diced mango, diced pineapple, dried cranberries, raisins, chopped nuts (such as almonds, walnuts, or pecans), sunflower seeds, pumpkin seeds, chocolate chips, coconut flakes, honey, and maple syrup.
3. Provide serving utensils: Place spoons or small scoops next to each topping to make it easy for guests to add them to their yogurt parfaits.
4. Create your own parfait: Invite guests to create their own yogurt parfaits by layering yogurt and toppings in individual bowls or cups. Encourage creativity and experimentation with different flavor combinations and layering techniques.
5. Enjoy! Once everyone has assembled their yogurt parfaits, they can dig in and enjoy the delicious and nutritious treats.

A yogurt parfait bar is perfect for breakfast, brunch, snacks, or even dessert. It's a fun and interactive way to enjoy a healthy and customizable meal together with friends and family. Plus, it's easy to set up and requires minimal preparation, making it a great option for gatherings of any size.

Homemade Applesauce

Ingredients:

- 6 medium-sized apples (any variety you like), peeled, cored, and chopped
- 1/2 cup water
- 2-4 tablespoons sugar (optional, depending on your preference and the sweetness of the apples)
- 1 teaspoon ground cinnamon (optional, for flavor)

Instructions:

1. Peel, core, and chop the apples into small chunks.
2. In a large saucepan, combine the chopped apples, water, sugar (if using), and cinnamon (if using). Stir to combine.
3. Place the saucepan over medium heat and bring the mixture to a simmer.
4. Reduce the heat to low and let the apples simmer, covered, for about 15-20 minutes, or until the apples are very soft and easily mashed with a fork.
5. Once the apples are soft, remove the saucepan from the heat.
6. Use a potato masher or a fork to mash the cooked apples until they reach your desired consistency. For a smoother applesauce, you can use an immersion blender or transfer the mixture to a blender or food processor and blend until smooth.
7. Taste the applesauce and adjust the sweetness and cinnamon to your liking, adding more sugar or cinnamon if desired.
8. Allow the applesauce to cool before transferring it to airtight containers or jars for storage.
9. Store the homemade applesauce in the refrigerator for up to 1 week, or freeze it in freezer-safe containers for longer storage.

Homemade applesauce is delicious served warm or chilled and makes a healthy and tasty snack or dessert. You can enjoy it on its own, or use it as a topping for oatmeal, pancakes, yogurt, or ice cream. Feel free to experiment with different apple varieties and flavorings to create your perfect applesauce recipe!

Veggie and Cheese Omelette

Ingredients:

- 3 large eggs
- 1/4 cup diced bell peppers (any color)
- 1/4 cup diced onions
- 1/4 cup sliced mushrooms
- 1/4 cup diced tomatoes
- 1/4 cup shredded cheese (cheddar, mozzarella, or your favorite cheese)
- Salt and pepper to taste
- 1 tablespoon olive oil or butter for cooking

Instructions:

1. In a mixing bowl, crack the eggs and beat them until well combined. Season with salt and pepper to taste.
2. Heat the olive oil or butter in a non-stick skillet over medium heat.
3. Add the diced bell peppers, onions, and mushrooms to the skillet. Sauté for 2-3 minutes, or until the vegetables are softened.
4. Pour the beaten eggs over the sautéed vegetables in the skillet. Allow the eggs to cook undisturbed for about 1-2 minutes, until the edges start to set.
5. Gently lift the edges of the omelette with a spatula and tilt the skillet to let the uncooked eggs flow to the bottom of the skillet.
6. Once the omelette is mostly set but still slightly runny on top, sprinkle the diced tomatoes and shredded cheese over one half of the omelette.
7. Using a spatula, fold the other half of the omelette over the side with the vegetables and cheese, creating a half-moon shape.
8. Cook the omelette for another 1-2 minutes, or until the cheese is melted and the eggs are cooked through.
9. Carefully slide the omelette onto a plate and cut it in half or into wedges.
10. Serve the veggie and cheese omelette hot, garnished with additional salt, pepper, or herbs if desired.

This veggie and cheese omelette is versatile and customizable, so feel free to experiment with different vegetables, cheeses, and seasonings to suit your taste preferences. It's a hearty and satisfying breakfast option that's packed with protein and nutrients to fuel your day!

Banana Sushi (banana rolled in peanut butter and cereal)

Ingredients:

- 1 medium ripe banana
- 2 tablespoons peanut butter (or any nut or seed butter of your choice)
- 1/4 cup crispy rice cereal or granola (choose your favorite variety)

Instructions:

1. Peel the banana and place it on a clean cutting board.
2. Spread a thin layer of peanut butter evenly over the entire surface of the banana.
3. Sprinkle the crispy rice cereal or granola over the peanut butter, pressing gently to ensure it sticks to the banana.
4. Carefully slice the banana into bite-sized pieces, about 1 inch thick, using a sharp knife.
5. Arrange the banana slices on a serving plate or tray, seam side down, so that the peanut butter and cereal are facing upward.
6. Repeat the process with the remaining banana slices until all are coated with peanut butter and cereal.
7. Serve the banana sushi immediately as a fun and nutritious snack or dessert option.

You can also get creative with your banana sushi by adding other toppings like chocolate chips, shredded coconut, or dried fruit before rolling it up. Feel free to experiment with different nut or seed butters and cereals to create your favorite flavor combinations. Enjoy the delicious and playful twist on traditional sushi!

Mini Meatball Subs

Ingredients:

- 1 pound ground beef (or a mixture of ground beef and pork)
- 1/2 cup breadcrumbs
- 1/4 cup grated Parmesan cheese
- 1 large egg
- 2 cloves garlic, minced
- 1 teaspoon dried oregano
- 1/2 teaspoon salt
- 1/4 teaspoon black pepper
- 1 tablespoon olive oil
- 1 cup marinara sauce
- Mini sub rolls or dinner rolls
- Shredded mozzarella cheese (optional)
- Fresh parsley, chopped (for garnish)

Instructions:

1. Preheat your oven to 400°F (200°C). Line a baking sheet with parchment paper or aluminum foil for easy cleanup.
2. In a large mixing bowl, combine the ground beef, breadcrumbs, grated Parmesan cheese, egg, minced garlic, dried oregano, salt, and black pepper. Use your hands or a spoon to mix until well combined.
3. Shape the meat mixture into small meatballs, about 1 inch in diameter. Place the meatballs on the prepared baking sheet, leaving some space between each one.
4. Heat the olive oil in a large skillet over medium heat. Add the meatballs in batches and cook until browned on all sides, about 5-7 minutes. Transfer the browned meatballs back to the baking sheet.
5. Once all the meatballs are browned, transfer the baking sheet to the preheated oven and bake for 10-12 minutes, or until the meatballs are cooked through.
6. While the meatballs are baking, heat the marinara sauce in a small saucepan over medium heat until warmed through.
7. Slice the mini sub rolls or dinner rolls in half horizontally. Place a few meatballs on the bottom half of each roll.
8. Spoon some marinara sauce over the meatballs, then sprinkle with shredded mozzarella cheese, if using.
9. Place the top half of each roll over the meatballs to form mini meatball subs.

10. Return the subs to the oven for a few minutes, just until the cheese is melted and the rolls are warmed through.
11. Remove the mini meatball subs from the oven and garnish with chopped fresh parsley.
12. Serve the mini meatball subs hot and enjoy!

These mini meatball subs are perfect for parties, game day snacks, or a fun family dinner. You can customize them with your favorite toppings or sauces to suit your taste. Enjoy the deliciousness!

Cheesy Broccoli Bites

Ingredients:

- 2 cups broccoli florets, chopped into small pieces
- 1 cup shredded cheddar cheese
- 1/4 cup grated Parmesan cheese
- 1/2 cup breadcrumbs
- 2 large eggs
- 2 cloves garlic, minced
- 1/2 teaspoon salt
- 1/4 teaspoon black pepper
- Cooking spray or olive oil, for greasing

Instructions:

1. Preheat your oven to 375°F (190°C). Grease a baking sheet with cooking spray or olive oil.
2. Steam the chopped broccoli florets until they are tender, about 5-7 minutes. Drain any excess water and let the broccoli cool slightly.
3. In a large mixing bowl, combine the cooked broccoli, shredded cheddar cheese, grated Parmesan cheese, breadcrumbs, eggs, minced garlic, salt, and black pepper. Mix until well combined.
4. Use a tablespoon or small ice cream scoop to portion out the broccoli mixture. Roll each portion into a ball and place it on the prepared baking sheet.
5. Use your fingers or the back of a spoon to flatten each broccoli ball slightly into a bite-sized disc.
6. Bake the cheesy broccoli bites in the preheated oven for 15-20 minutes, or until they are golden brown and crispy on the outside.
7. Remove the baking sheet from the oven and let the cheesy broccoli bites cool for a few minutes before serving.
8. Serve the cheesy broccoli bites warm as a snack or appetizer. You can enjoy them on their own or with your favorite dipping sauce, such as marinara sauce, ranch dressing, or aioli.

These cheesy broccoli bites are packed with flavor and nutrients, making them a delicious and wholesome snack option. They're also a great way to sneak some extra veggies into your diet. Enjoy!

English Muffin Pizzas

Ingredients:

- English muffins, split in half
- Pizza sauce
- Shredded mozzarella cheese
- Toppings of your choice (such as pepperoni, sliced bell peppers, onions, mushrooms, olives, etc.)
- Optional: dried herbs (such as oregano, basil, or red pepper flakes)

Instructions:

1. Preheat your oven to 375°F (190°C). Line a baking sheet with parchment paper or aluminum foil for easy cleanup.
2. Place the English muffin halves on the prepared baking sheet, cut side up.
3. Spread a spoonful of pizza sauce over each English muffin half, covering the surface evenly.
4. Sprinkle shredded mozzarella cheese over the pizza sauce, covering the English muffin halves to your desired level of cheesiness.
5. Add your favorite toppings over the cheese layer. Get creative and customize each English muffin pizza with different toppings according to your preferences.
6. If desired, sprinkle dried herbs over the top of the pizzas for added flavor.
7. Place the baking sheet in the preheated oven and bake the English muffin pizzas for 10-12 minutes, or until the cheese is melted and bubbly, and the edges of the English muffins are golden brown.
8. Remove the baking sheet from the oven and let the English muffin pizzas cool for a few minutes before serving.
9. Serve the English muffin pizzas warm as a delicious snack, appetizer, or quick meal option. Enjoy!

These English muffin pizzas are versatile and customizable, making them a great option for busy weeknights or casual gatherings. You can easily adjust the toppings to suit your taste preferences or use whatever ingredients you have on hand. Have fun creating and enjoying your own mini pizzas!

Turkey and Cheese Roll-Ups

Ingredients:

- Thinly sliced deli turkey breast
- Sliced cheese (cheddar, Swiss, provolone, or your favorite cheese)
- Lettuce leaves (optional)
- Mayonnaise or mustard (optional)
- Toothpicks or small skewers

Instructions:

1. Lay out a slice of deli turkey breast on a clean work surface.
2. Place a slice of cheese on top of the turkey slice. If desired, add a lettuce leaf and a small amount of mayonnaise or mustard on top of the cheese.
3. Starting from one end, tightly roll up the turkey slice with the cheese and any additional toppings inside.
4. Once rolled, secure the roll-up with a toothpick or small skewer to hold it together.
5. Repeat the process with the remaining turkey slices, cheese, and toppings until you have made the desired number of roll-ups.
6. Serve the turkey and cheese roll-ups immediately as a snack or light meal. They can be enjoyed on their own or paired with crackers, raw veggies, or a side salad.

These turkey and cheese roll-ups are versatile, customizable, and perfect for a quick and protein-packed snack or meal. You can also experiment with different types of deli meats, cheeses, and toppings to create your favorite flavor combinations. Enjoy!

No-Bake Energy Bites

Ingredients:

- 1 cup old-fashioned rolled oats
- 1/2 cup nut butter (such as peanut butter, almond butter, or cashew butter)
- 1/4 cup honey or maple syrup
- 1/4 cup ground flaxseed or chia seeds
- 1/4 cup mini chocolate chips or chopped nuts (optional)
- 1 teaspoon vanilla extract
- Pinch of salt

Instructions:

1. In a large mixing bowl, combine the rolled oats, nut butter, honey or maple syrup, ground flaxseed or chia seeds, mini chocolate chips or chopped nuts (if using), vanilla extract, and a pinch of salt.
2. Stir the ingredients together until well combined. If the mixture seems too dry, you can add a little more honey or nut butter to help bind it together.
3. Once the mixture is well combined, cover the bowl and refrigerate it for about 30 minutes to allow it to firm up slightly.
4. After chilling, remove the mixture from the refrigerator. Use a spoon or cookie scoop to portion out small amounts of the mixture and roll them into bite-sized balls using your hands.
5. Place the energy bites on a baking sheet lined with parchment paper or wax paper.
6. Once all the mixture has been rolled into balls, transfer the baking sheet to the refrigerator and let the energy bites chill for at least 1 hour to firm up.
7. Once chilled, the energy bites are ready to enjoy! Store any leftovers in an airtight container in the refrigerator for up to one week.

These no-bake energy bites are customizable, so feel free to experiment with different add-ins like dried fruit, coconut flakes, or protein powder to suit your taste preferences. They're a great snack option for busy days, post-workout fuel, or satisfying sweet cravings in a healthier way. Enjoy!

Fruit and Cheese Skewers

Ingredients:

- Assorted fruits (such as grapes, strawberries, pineapple chunks, melon cubes, kiwi slices, or any other fruits of your choice)
- Assorted cheese cubes (such as cheddar, mozzarella, Colby jack, or Swiss cheese)
- Wooden skewers or toothpicks

Instructions:

1. Wash and prepare the fruits by slicing or cutting them into bite-sized pieces. Cut the cheese into cubes of a similar size.
2. Thread the fruit and cheese alternately onto the wooden skewers or toothpicks, creating colorful and flavorful combinations.
3. Continue threading the fruit and cheese onto the skewers until you reach the desired amount. You can mix and match different fruits and cheeses to create a variety of skewers.
4. Arrange the fruit and cheese skewers on a serving platter or tray, placing them in a decorative pattern for presentation.
5. Serve the fruit and cheese skewers immediately as a tasty appetizer or snack. They can be enjoyed on their own or paired with a dipping sauce or yogurt dip.

These fruit and cheese skewers are not only delicious but also visually appealing, making them a hit with both kids and adults. They're a great way to incorporate more fruits and calcium-rich cheese into your diet while enjoying a fun and portable snack. Feel free to get creative with different fruit and cheese combinations to suit your taste preferences. Enjoy!

Pancake Dippers with Fruit

Ingredients:

- Pancake batter (you can use your favorite pancake recipe or a store-bought mix)
- Assorted fruits (such as strawberries, bananas, blueberries, raspberries, or any other fruits of your choice), washed, peeled, and sliced
- Maple syrup or honey, for dipping

Instructions:

1. Prepare the pancake batter according to the instructions on the package or your favorite recipe. Make sure the batter is smooth and free of lumps.
2. Preheat a non-stick skillet or griddle over medium heat. Lightly grease the skillet with butter or cooking spray.
3. Pour small circles of pancake batter onto the skillet, spacing them a few inches apart. You can make mini pancakes or use a pancake mold to create uniform shapes, such as hearts or circles.
4. Place a few slices of fruit onto each pancake while the first side cooks. You can press them gently into the batter to help them stick.
5. Once bubbles start to form on the surface of the pancakes and the edges begin to set, carefully flip them using a spatula.
6. Cook the pancakes for an additional 1-2 minutes on the other side, or until they are golden brown and cooked through.
7. Remove the cooked pancake dippers from the skillet and transfer them to a serving plate.
8. Serve the pancake dippers with fruit immediately, accompanied by maple syrup or honey for dipping.

These pancake dippers with fruit are not only delicious but also interactive and fun to eat. They're perfect for kids and adults alike and make a delightful addition to any breakfast or brunch spread. Feel free to get creative with different fruit combinations and pancake shapes to suit your taste preferences. Enjoy!

Rice Cake Toppings Bar

Ingredients:

- Rice cakes (plain or flavored)
- Assorted toppings (sweet and savory options):
    - Nut butter (peanut butter, almond butter, cashew butter)
    - Jam or fruit preserves
    - Sliced fruits (bananas, strawberries, blueberries, apples)
    - Sliced vegetables (cucumber, avocado, tomato)
    - Cheese slices or shredded cheese
    - Hummus
    - Sliced deli meats (turkey, ham, chicken)
    - Smoked salmon or canned tuna
    - Sliced hard-boiled eggs
    - Honey or maple syrup
    - Chocolate chips or chocolate spread
    - Sprinkles or shredded coconut
    - Herbs and spices (cilantro, basil, red pepper flakes)
    - Salt and pepper

Instructions:

1. Arrange the rice cakes on a large platter or tray, leaving space between each one.
2. Set out small bowls or containers for each topping, placing them around the rice cakes.
3. Fill each bowl or container with a different topping, making sure to include a variety of sweet and savory options.
4. Provide spreading utensils, such as butter knives or small spoons, for guests to use when adding toppings to their rice cakes.
5. Encourage guests to create their own rice cake masterpieces by layering different toppings on top of the rice cakes.
6. Have fun experimenting with flavor combinations and building unique creations!
7. Serve the rice cake toppings bar as a snack, appetizer, or light meal option for parties, gatherings, or family fun nights.

A rice cake toppings bar is a versatile and customizable option that allows everyone to create their own personalized snacks. It's a great way to accommodate different taste preferences and dietary restrictions while fostering creativity and enjoyment. Enjoy exploring the endless possibilities of rice cake toppings!

Taco Cups

Ingredients:

- 1 pound ground beef or turkey
- 1 packet taco seasoning mix
- 1 (10-ounce) can diced tomatoes with green chilies, drained
- 1 cup shredded cheddar cheese
- 24 wonton wrappers
- Optional toppings: diced tomatoes, sliced black olives, diced avocado, sour cream, salsa, chopped cilantro, etc.

Instructions:

1. Preheat your oven to 375°F (190°C). Lightly grease a muffin tin with cooking spray.
2. In a skillet over medium heat, cook the ground beef or turkey until browned and cooked through, breaking it up with a spoon as it cooks.
3. Drain any excess fat from the skillet, then add the taco seasoning mix and diced tomatoes with green chilies. Stir to combine and cook for a few more minutes until heated through.
4. Place one wonton wrapper into each muffin cup, pressing gently to form a cup shape.
5. Spoon a small amount of the taco meat mixture into each wonton cup, filling it about halfway.
6. Sprinkle shredded cheddar cheese over the taco meat in each cup.
7. Place another wonton wrapper on top of the cheese layer in each cup, pressing gently to adhere.
8. Repeat the process with the remaining wonton wrappers, taco meat mixture, and cheese, until all the muffin cups are filled.
9. Bake the taco cups in the preheated oven for 10-12 minutes, or until the wonton wrappers are golden brown and crispy, and the cheese is melted and bubbly.
10. Remove the muffin tin from the oven and let the taco cups cool for a few minutes before serving.
11. Carefully remove the taco cups from the muffin tin using a spoon or fork and transfer them to a serving platter.
12. Serve the taco cups hot, garnished with your favorite toppings such as diced tomatoes, sliced black olives, diced avocado, sour cream, salsa, and chopped cilantro.

These taco cups are perfect for parties, game day snacks, or a fun weeknight dinner option. They're easy to customize with your favorite taco toppings and are sure to be a hit with family and friends. Enjoy!

Mini Bagel Pizzas

Ingredients:

- Mini bagels, sliced in half
- Pizza sauce
- Shredded mozzarella cheese
- Assorted toppings (such as pepperoni slices, sliced bell peppers, sliced mushrooms, sliced olives, etc.)
- Optional: dried herbs (such as oregano, basil, or red pepper flakes)

Instructions:

1. Preheat your oven to 375°F (190°C). Line a baking sheet with parchment paper or aluminum foil for easy cleanup.
2. Place the mini bagel halves on the prepared baking sheet, cut side up.
3. Spread a spoonful of pizza sauce over each bagel half, covering the surface evenly.
4. Sprinkle shredded mozzarella cheese over the pizza sauce, covering the bagel halves to your desired level of cheesiness.
5. Add your favorite toppings over the cheese layer. Get creative and customize each mini bagel pizza with different toppings according to your preferences.
6. If desired, sprinkle dried herbs over the top of the pizzas for added flavor.
7. Place the baking sheet in the preheated oven and bake the mini bagel pizzas for 10-12 minutes, or until the cheese is melted and bubbly, and the edges of the bagels are golden brown.
8. Remove the baking sheet from the oven and let the mini bagel pizzas cool for a few minutes before serving.
9. Serve the mini bagel pizzas hot as a tasty snack or meal. They can be enjoyed on their own or paired with a side salad or vegetable sticks for a complete meal.

These mini bagel pizzas are versatile and customizable, making them a great option for busy weeknights or casual gatherings. You can easily adjust the toppings to suit your taste preferences or use whatever ingredients you have on hand. Enjoy creating and eating these delicious mini pizzas!

Apple Nachos (sliced apples topped with peanut butter and granola)

Ingredients:

- 2 medium apples, cored and thinly sliced
- 1/4 cup peanut butter or almond butter
- 1/4 cup granola (choose your favorite variety)
- Optional toppings: chocolate chips, shredded coconut, chopped nuts, dried fruit, honey, maple syrup, cinnamon, etc.

Instructions:

1. Arrange the sliced apples in a single layer on a serving platter or large plate.
2. Warm the peanut butter or almond butter in the microwave for a few seconds until it becomes smooth and easy to drizzle.
3. Drizzle the warm peanut butter or almond butter evenly over the sliced apples.
4. Sprinkle the granola over the apples, distributing it evenly to cover the surface.
5. Add any optional toppings of your choice, such as chocolate chips, shredded coconut, chopped nuts, or dried fruit.
6. If desired, drizzle a little honey or maple syrup over the top for extra sweetness.
7. Finish with a sprinkle of cinnamon for added flavor, if desired.
8. Serve the apple nachos immediately as a delicious and nutritious snack or dessert.

Apple nachos are best enjoyed fresh, but you can also prepare the sliced apples and toppings ahead of time and assemble them just before serving to prevent them from becoming soggy. Get creative with your toppings and customize the apple nachos to suit your taste preferences. They're a fun and wholesome treat that's sure to be a hit with kids and adults alike!

Veggie and Hummus Wraps

Ingredients:

- Tortillas or wraps (whole wheat, spinach, or your favorite variety)
- Hummus (store-bought or homemade)
- Assorted vegetables (such as lettuce, spinach, sliced cucumbers, shredded carrots, bell peppers, avocado, sprouts, etc.)
- Optional additions: sliced cheese, cooked quinoa, cooked chickpeas, sliced olives, sun-dried tomatoes, etc.
- Optional seasonings: salt, pepper, garlic powder, lemon juice, balsamic vinegar, etc.

Instructions:

1. Lay out a tortilla or wrap on a clean work surface.
2. Spread a generous layer of hummus evenly over the entire surface of the tortilla.
3. Layer your choice of vegetables and optional additions on top of the hummus, placing them in the center of the tortilla.
4. If desired, sprinkle any optional seasonings or drizzle sauces over the vegetables for added flavor.
5. Carefully fold the sides of the tortilla inward, then roll it up tightly from the bottom to create a wrap.
6. Repeat the process with the remaining tortillas and fillings until all the wraps are assembled.
7. If serving immediately, you can slice the wraps in half diagonally for easier eating. Otherwise, you can wrap them tightly in plastic wrap or foil and refrigerate them until ready to serve.
8. Serve the veggie and hummus wraps as a nutritious and satisfying meal or snack.

These veggie and hummus wraps are versatile and customizable, so feel free to experiment with different combinations of vegetables, hummus flavors, and optional additions to suit your taste preferences. They're perfect for packing in lunchboxes, taking on picnics, or enjoying on the go. Enjoy!

DIY Smoothie Bowls

Ingredients:

- Frozen fruit (such as berries, bananas, mango, pineapple, etc.)
- Fresh fruit (such as berries, bananas, kiwi, etc.)
- Leafy greens (such as spinach or kale)
- Liquid (such as water, coconut water, milk, or fruit juice)
- Optional add-ins (such as protein powder, nut butter, chia seeds, flaxseeds, oats, yogurt, etc.)
- Toppings (such as granola, sliced almonds, shredded coconut, chia seeds, hemp seeds, sliced fruit, etc.)

Instructions:

1. Choose your base ingredients: Start by selecting a combination of frozen fruit, fresh fruit, and leafy greens for the base of your smoothie bowl. You can use any combination of fruits and greens that you like, depending on your taste preferences and what you have available.
2. Blend the base ingredients: In a blender, combine the frozen fruit, fresh fruit, leafy greens, and liquid of your choice. Start with a small amount of liquid and add more as needed to achieve your desired consistency. Blend until smooth and creamy.
3. Customize your smoothie bowl: Once the base is blended, you can add any optional add-ins to enhance the flavor and nutrition of your smoothie bowl. This could include protein powder for extra protein, nut butter for creaminess and flavor, chia seeds or flaxseeds for added fiber and omega-3 fatty acids, oats for thickness and texture, or yogurt for probiotics.
4. Pour the smoothie into a bowl: Transfer the blended smoothie mixture into a bowl.
5. Add your favorite toppings: Decorate your smoothie bowl with a variety of toppings to add texture, flavor, and visual appeal. Some popular topping options include granola, sliced almonds, shredded coconut, chia seeds, hemp seeds, sliced fruit, or drizzles of nut butter or honey.
6. Enjoy your DIY smoothie bowl: Grab a spoon and dig in! Enjoy your delicious and nutritious creation as a satisfying breakfast, snack, or even dessert.

Smoothie bowls are highly customizable, so feel free to experiment with different flavor combinations, textures, and toppings to create your perfect bowl. Have fun getting creative and enjoy the nutritious goodness of your DIY smoothie bowl!

Grilled Cheese Roll-Ups

Ingredients:

- Sliced bread (white, whole wheat, or your favorite variety)
- Sliced cheese (cheddar, American, Swiss, or your favorite cheese)
- Butter or margarine, softened
- Optional fillings: cooked bacon, sliced ham, sliced turkey, tomato slices, avocado slices, etc.

Instructions:

1. Flatten the slices of bread using a rolling pin or the palm of your hand to make them easier to roll up.
2. Place a slice of cheese on each slice of bread, leaving a small border around the edges.
3. If using any optional fillings, place them on top of the cheese in a single layer.
4. Starting from one end, tightly roll up each slice of bread with the cheese and fillings inside, like a jelly roll.
5. Heat a non-stick skillet or griddle over medium heat.
6. Spread a thin layer of softened butter or margarine on the outside of each rolled-up sandwich.
7. Place the rolled-up sandwiches seam side down in the preheated skillet or griddle.
8. Cook the rolled-up sandwiches for 2-3 minutes on each side, or until they are golden brown and crispy on the outside and the cheese is melted and gooey on the inside.
9. Remove the grilled cheese roll-ups from the skillet or griddle and let them cool for a minute or two before serving.
10. Slice the grilled cheese roll-ups diagonally into bite-sized pieces, if desired.
11. Serve the grilled cheese roll-ups warm as a fun and delicious snack or meal. Enjoy them on their own or with your favorite dipping sauce, such as marinara sauce or ranch dressing.

Grilled cheese roll-ups are a tasty and versatile dish that's sure to be a hit with kids and adults alike. Feel free to customize them with your favorite cheese and fillings to suit your taste preferences. Enjoy!

Fruit and Yogurt Popsicles

Ingredients:

- 1 cup plain or vanilla yogurt (Greek yogurt or regular yogurt)
- 1 cup mixed fresh or frozen fruits (such as berries, mango chunks, pineapple chunks, sliced peaches, etc.)
- 1-2 tablespoons honey or maple syrup (optional, for added sweetness)
- Popsicle molds
- Popsicle sticks

Instructions:

1. In a blender or food processor, combine the yogurt, mixed fruits, and honey or maple syrup (if using). Blend until smooth and well combined. Taste the mixture and adjust the sweetness if necessary.
2. Pour the fruit and yogurt mixture into popsicle molds, filling each mold to the top.
3. If your popsicle molds have slots for popsicle sticks, insert the sticks into the molds. If not, you can place a piece of aluminum foil over the top of the molds and insert the sticks through the foil to keep them upright.
4. Tap the molds gently on the countertop to remove any air bubbles and ensure that the mixture is evenly distributed.
5. Place the popsicle molds in the freezer and freeze for at least 4-6 hours, or until the popsicles are completely frozen.
6. Once the popsicles are frozen solid, remove them from the molds by running warm water over the outside of the molds for a few seconds to loosen the popsicles. Gently pull the popsicles out of the molds and enjoy immediately.
7. If you're not serving the popsicles right away, you can wrap them individually in plastic wrap or store them in a resealable plastic bag in the freezer for later.

These fruit and yogurt popsicles are a delicious and healthy alternative to store-bought popsicles, and you can customize them with your favorite fruits and yogurt flavors. They're perfect for cooling off on a hot day and make a great snack or dessert for kids and adults alike. Enjoy!

Baked Zucchini Fries

Ingredients:

- 2 medium zucchinis
- 1/2 cup all-purpose flour (or almond flour for a gluten-free option)
- 2 large eggs
- 1 cup breadcrumbs (or panko breadcrumbs for extra crispiness)
- 1/4 cup grated Parmesan cheese
- 1 teaspoon garlic powder
- 1 teaspoon paprika
- 1/2 teaspoon salt
- 1/4 teaspoon black pepper
- Cooking spray or olive oil

Instructions:

1. Preheat your oven to 425°F (220°C). Line a baking sheet with parchment paper or aluminum foil and lightly grease with cooking spray or olive oil.
2. Wash the zucchinis and cut off the ends. Slice each zucchini lengthwise into thin strips, about 1/2 inch wide, to resemble fries.
3. In a shallow dish, place the flour. In another shallow dish, beat the eggs. In a third shallow dish, combine the breadcrumbs, grated Parmesan cheese, garlic powder, paprika, salt, and black pepper.
4. Dredge each zucchini fry in the flour, shaking off any excess. Then dip it into the beaten eggs, allowing any excess to drip off. Finally, coat it evenly in the breadcrumb mixture, pressing gently to adhere.
5. Place the coated zucchini fries on the prepared baking sheet in a single layer, leaving space between each fry.
6. Lightly spray the tops of the zucchini fries with cooking spray or drizzle them with olive oil for extra crispiness.
7. Bake the zucchini fries in the preheated oven for 20-25 minutes, flipping halfway through, or until they are golden brown and crispy.
8. Remove the baking sheet from the oven and let the zucchini fries cool for a few minutes before serving.
9. Serve the baked zucchini fries hot with your favorite dipping sauce, such as marinara sauce, ranch dressing, or tzatziki.

These baked zucchini fries are a tasty and nutritious snack or side dish that's sure to be a hit with the whole family. They're crispy on the outside, tender on the inside, and packed with flavor. Enjoy!

DIY Sushi Rolls (using cucumber, avocado, and cream cheese)

Ingredients:

- Sushi rice (short-grain rice)
- Nori (seaweed) sheets
- Cucumber, thinly sliced into strips
- Avocado, sliced
- Cream cheese, softened
- Soy sauce, for dipping (optional)
- Pickled ginger and wasabi, for serving (optional)

Instructions:

1. Cook the sushi rice according to the package instructions. Once cooked, let the rice cool slightly.
2. Place a sheet of nori on a bamboo sushi mat or a clean kitchen towel.
3. Moisten your hands with water to prevent the rice from sticking, then spread a thin layer of sushi rice evenly over the nori sheet, leaving about 1 inch of space at the top edge.
4. Arrange strips of cucumber, avocado slices, and small dollops of cream cheese in a line across the center of the rice.
5. Starting from the bottom edge closest to you, carefully roll the sushi mat or kitchen towel away from you, enclosing the filling.
6. Continue rolling, applying gentle pressure to shape the sushi roll.
7. Once rolled, use a sharp knife to slice the sushi roll into individual pieces, about 1 inch thick.
8. Repeat the process with the remaining nori sheets and filling ingredients.
9. Serve the DIY sushi rolls with soy sauce for dipping, and optionally with pickled ginger and wasabi on the side.
10. Enjoy your homemade sushi rolls as a delicious snack or light meal!

These DIY sushi rolls are customizable, so feel free to experiment with different fillings and toppings to suit your taste preferences. You can also get creative with sauces like spicy mayo or eel sauce for added flavor. Have fun making and enjoying your homemade sushi!

Turkey and Veggie Pinwheels

Ingredients:

- Tortillas or wraps (whole wheat, spinach, or your favorite variety)
- Sliced turkey breast
- Cream cheese or hummus
- Assorted vegetables, thinly sliced (such as bell peppers, cucumbers, carrots, spinach, etc.)
- Optional: shredded cheese, sprouts, avocado slices, etc.

Instructions:

1. Lay out a tortilla or wrap on a clean work surface.
2. Spread a layer of cream cheese or hummus evenly over the entire surface of the tortilla.
3. Arrange slices of turkey breast in a single layer on top of the cream cheese or hummus.
4. Place a variety of thinly sliced vegetables on top of the turkey, covering the surface evenly.
5. If desired, sprinkle shredded cheese over the vegetables for extra flavor.
6. Starting from one end, tightly roll up the tortilla, enclosing the filling inside like a jelly roll.
7. Once rolled, use a sharp knife to slice the tortilla into individual pinwheels, about 1 inch thick.
8. Repeat the process with the remaining tortillas and filling ingredients.
9. Arrange the turkey and veggie pinwheels on a serving platter and secure each pinwheel with a toothpick to hold it together, if necessary.
10. Serve the pinwheels immediately as a delicious and nutritious snack or appetizer.

These turkey and veggie pinwheels are versatile and customizable, so feel free to experiment with different fillings and flavors to suit your taste preferences. They're perfect for parties, potlucks, or lunchboxes, and are sure to be a hit with both kids and adults alike. Enjoy!

Baked Chicken Tenders

Ingredients:

- 1 pound chicken tenders or boneless, skinless chicken breasts, cut into strips
- 1 cup breadcrumbs (plain or seasoned)
- 1/4 cup grated Parmesan cheese
- 1 teaspoon garlic powder
- 1 teaspoon paprika
- 1/2 teaspoon salt
- 1/4 teaspoon black pepper
- 2 large eggs, beaten
- Cooking spray or olive oil

Instructions:

1. Preheat your oven to 400°F (200°C). Line a baking sheet with parchment paper or aluminum foil and lightly grease with cooking spray or olive oil.
2. In a shallow dish, combine the breadcrumbs, grated Parmesan cheese, garlic powder, paprika, salt, and black pepper. Stir until well mixed.
3. Place the beaten eggs in another shallow dish.
4. Dip each chicken tender into the beaten eggs, coating it evenly.
5. Then, dredge the chicken tender in the breadcrumb mixture, pressing gently to adhere the breadcrumbs to the chicken.
6. Place the coated chicken tenders on the prepared baking sheet, leaving space between each tender.
7. Lightly spray the tops of the chicken tenders with cooking spray or drizzle them with olive oil for extra crispiness.
8. Bake the chicken tenders in the preheated oven for 15-20 minutes, or until they are golden brown and cooked through, with an internal temperature of 165°F (75°C).
9. Remove the baking sheet from the oven and let the chicken tenders cool for a few minutes before serving.
10. Serve the baked chicken tenders hot with your favorite dipping sauce, such as barbecue sauce, honey mustard, or ranch dressing.

These baked chicken tenders are crispy on the outside and juicy on the inside, and they're perfect for serving as a main dish or appetizer. They're also customizable, so feel free to experiment with different seasonings and coatings to suit your taste preferences. Enjoy!

Cheese and Crackers Snack Platter

Ingredients:

- Assorted cheeses (such as cheddar, Swiss, brie, goat cheese, gouda, etc.), sliced or cubed
- Assorted crackers (such as water crackers, wheat crackers, multigrain crackers, etc.)
- Optional: sliced cured meats (such as salami, prosciutto, or pepperoni), olives, nuts, dried fruits, fresh fruits (such as grapes or apple slices), honey or jam for drizzling, mustard or chutney for dipping, etc.

Instructions:

1. Start by selecting a variety of cheeses to feature on your platter. Choose a mix of soft, semi-soft, and hard cheeses to provide a range of flavors and textures. Arrange the cheese slices or cubes on a large serving platter or cheese board, leaving space between each type of cheese.
2. Next, add a selection of crackers to the platter. Choose crackers that complement the flavors of the cheeses you've selected. Arrange the crackers around the cheese, filling in any gaps on the platter.
3. If desired, add sliced cured meats to the platter. Place them in between the cheese and crackers or in a separate section of the platter.
4. Enhance the platter with additional accompaniments such as olives, nuts, dried fruits, and fresh fruits. Scatter them around the cheese and crackers for visual appeal.
5. For added flavor and presentation, drizzle honey or jam over some of the cheeses, or serve mustard or chutney on the side for dipping.
6. Once assembled, garnish the platter with fresh herbs or edible flowers for an extra touch of elegance.
7. Serve the cheese and crackers platter at room temperature, allowing the flavors of the cheeses to fully develop. Provide small cheese knives or spreaders for guests to use when serving themselves.
8. Encourage guests to mix and match different cheese and cracker combinations to discover their favorite flavor pairings.

A cheese and crackers snack platter is perfect for entertaining guests at parties, gatherings, or wine tastings, and it's also a great option for a simple yet elegant snack at home. Enjoy!

Veggie Chips (baked slices of sweet potato, zucchini, or carrot)

Ingredients:

- Sweet potatoes, zucchini, or carrots (or a combination of these vegetables)
- Olive oil or avocado oil
- Salt and pepper, to taste
- Optional seasonings: garlic powder, paprika, cumin, chili powder, etc.

Instructions:

1. Preheat your oven to 375°F (190°C). Line a baking sheet with parchment paper or aluminum foil for easy cleanup.
2. Wash and peel the vegetables (if desired). Using a sharp knife or a mandoline slicer, thinly slice the vegetables into uniform rounds, about 1/8 inch thick. Try to make the slices as uniform as possible to ensure even cooking.
3. Place the sliced vegetables in a large mixing bowl. Drizzle them with olive oil or avocado oil, tossing to coat evenly.
4. Season the vegetables with salt, pepper, and any additional seasonings of your choice, such as garlic powder, paprika, cumin, or chili powder. Toss to coat evenly.
5. Arrange the seasoned vegetable slices in a single layer on the prepared baking sheet, making sure they are not overlapping.
6. Bake the veggie chips in the preheated oven for 15-20 minutes, flipping halfway through, or until they are golden brown and crispy around the edges.
7. Keep an eye on the veggie chips towards the end of the baking time to prevent them from burning. The cooking time may vary depending on the thickness of the vegetable slices and your oven.
8. Once the veggie chips are done baking, remove them from the oven and let them cool on the baking sheet for a few minutes.
9. Serve the baked veggie chips warm as a healthy and satisfying snack. Enjoy them on their own or with your favorite dip, such as hummus, guacamole, or Greek yogurt dip.

These baked veggie chips are crispy, flavorful, and packed with nutrients, making them a great alternative to store-bought chips. Feel free to customize the seasonings to suit your taste preferences, and experiment with different vegetables for variety. Enjoy!

Mini Corn Dog Muffins

Ingredients:

- 1 cup cornmeal
- 1 cup all-purpose flour
- 1/4 cup granulated sugar
- 1 tablespoon baking powder
- 1/2 teaspoon salt
- 1 cup milk
- 1/4 cup vegetable oil
- 2 large eggs
- 8-10 hot dogs, cut into 1-inch pieces
- Cooking spray

Instructions:

1. Preheat your oven to 400°F (200°C). Grease a mini muffin tin with cooking spray or line it with mini muffin liners.
2. In a large mixing bowl, whisk together the cornmeal, flour, sugar, baking powder, and salt until well combined.
3. In a separate bowl, whisk together the milk, vegetable oil, and eggs until smooth.
4. Pour the wet ingredients into the dry ingredients and stir until just combined. Be careful not to overmix.
5. Spoon the cornbread batter into the prepared mini muffin tin, filling each cup about halfway full.
6. Place a piece of hot dog into the center of each muffin cup, pressing it down slightly into the batter.
7. Bake the mini corn dog muffins in the preheated oven for 10-12 minutes, or until they are golden brown and cooked through.
8. Remove the muffin tin from the oven and let the mini corn dog muffins cool for a few minutes before serving.
9. Once cooled slightly, remove the mini corn dog muffins from the muffin tin and transfer them to a serving platter.
10. Serve the mini corn dog muffins warm with your favorite dipping sauce, such as ketchup, mustard, or barbecue sauce.

These mini corn dog muffins are sure to be a hit with kids and adults alike. They're portable, easy to eat, and packed with classic corn dog flavor. Enjoy!

Peanut Butter and Jelly Sushi Rolls

Ingredients:

- 2 slices of sandwich bread (white, whole wheat, or your favorite variety)
- Peanut butter
- Jelly or jam (grape, strawberry, raspberry, etc.)
- Optional: sliced banana or other fruits

Instructions:

1. Using a rolling pin, flatten each slice of bread until it is thin and slightly flattened.
2. Spread a thin layer of peanut butter evenly over each slice of flattened bread.
3. Spoon a thin line of jelly or jam along one edge of each slice of bread.
4. If using, place a line of sliced banana or other fruits next to the jelly or jam.
5. Starting from the edge with the peanut butter and jelly, carefully roll up each slice of bread into a tight spiral, like a sushi roll.
6. Once rolled up, use a sharp knife to slice each roll into bite-sized pieces, about 1 inch thick.
7. Arrange the peanut butter and jelly sushi rolls on a serving platter and serve immediately.

These peanut butter and jelly sushi rolls are a fun and tasty snack that's perfect for kids and adults alike. They're great for lunchboxes, after-school snacks, or as a creative twist on a classic favorite. Enjoy!

Carrot and Hummus Snack Packs

Ingredients:

- Baby carrots
- Hummus (store-bought or homemade)
- Small plastic cups or containers with lids
- Optional: sliced cucumber, celery sticks, bell pepper strips, cherry tomatoes, etc.

Instructions:

1. Wash and dry the baby carrots and any additional vegetables you plan to include in the snack packs.
2. Divide the baby carrots and any other vegetables evenly among the small plastic cups or containers.
3. Spoon a portion of hummus into each cup or container, leaving space at the top for dipping.
4. Seal the lids on the cups or containers to keep the hummus fresh and prevent leaks.
5. If you're using reusable containers, pack them in an insulated lunch bag or cooler with an ice pack to keep them chilled until ready to eat.
6. If you're making the snack packs ahead of time, store them in the refrigerator until ready to enjoy.
7. When you're ready to eat, simply open the container, dip the baby carrots and vegetables into the hummus, and enjoy!

These carrot and hummus snack packs are not only delicious and convenient but also packed with nutrients. They're perfect for satisfying hunger between meals or as a healthy snack option for work, school, or travel. Feel free to customize the snack packs with your favorite vegetables or additional toppings like olives or pita chips. Enjoy!

Baked Apple Chips

Ingredients:

- Apples (any variety you like)
- Cinnamon (optional, for added flavor)

Instructions:

1. Preheat your oven to 200°F (95°C). Line a baking sheet with parchment paper or a silicone baking mat.
2. Wash and dry the apples thoroughly. You can peel the apples if you prefer, but leaving the peel on adds extra fiber and nutrients.
3. Using a sharp knife or a mandoline slicer, slice the apples thinly, about 1/8 inch thick. Try to make the slices as uniform as possible to ensure even baking.
4. Arrange the apple slices in a single layer on the prepared baking sheet, making sure they are not overlapping.
5. If desired, sprinkle the apple slices with cinnamon for added flavor.
6. Bake the apple slices in the preheated oven for 1.5 to 2 hours, flipping them halfway through, or until they are crisp and golden brown.
7. Keep an eye on the apple chips towards the end of the baking time to prevent them from burning. The baking time may vary depending on the thickness of the apple slices and your oven.
8. Once the apple chips are done baking, remove them from the oven and let them cool on the baking sheet for a few minutes.
9. Transfer the baked apple chips to a wire rack to cool completely. They will continue to crisp up as they cool.
10. Store the baked apple chips in an airtight container at room temperature for up to a week. Enjoy them as a healthy snack on their own, or pair them with yogurt, nut butter, or cheese for added flavor.

These baked apple chips are crispy, sweet, and addictive, making them a great alternative to store-bought chips. They're perfect for satisfying your sweet cravings in a healthier way. Enjoy!

Mini Quiches

Ingredients:

- Pie crust (store-bought or homemade)
- Eggs (about 4-5 large eggs)
- Milk or heavy cream (about 1/2 cup)
- Salt and pepper to taste
- Fillings (such as cooked bacon or ham, sautéed vegetables, cheese, herbs, etc.)

Instructions:

1. Preheat your oven to 375°F (190°C). Grease a mini muffin tin or line it with mini muffin liners.
2. Roll out the pie crust on a lightly floured surface. Using a round cookie cutter or glass, cut out circles of dough slightly larger than the openings in the mini muffin tin.
3. Press the circles of dough into the bottom of each mini muffin cup, forming small tart shells.
4. In a mixing bowl, whisk together the eggs, milk or cream, salt, and pepper until well combined.
5. Add your desired fillings to each mini muffin cup. You can mix and match fillings to create different flavor combinations.
6. Pour the egg mixture over the fillings in each mini muffin cup, filling them almost to the top.
7. Bake the mini quiches in the preheated oven for 15-20 minutes, or until they are set and golden brown on top.
8. Remove the mini quiches from the oven and let them cool in the muffin tin for a few minutes before transferring them to a wire rack to cool completely.
9. Serve the mini quiches warm or at room temperature as a delicious appetizer, snack, or breakfast option.

These mini quiches are versatile and can be customized with your favorite fillings. They're perfect for parties, brunches, or any occasion where you want to impress with a homemade treat. Enjoy!

DIY Fruit Leather

Ingredients:

- 4 cups of chopped fruit (such as strawberries, apples, peaches, mangoes, or a combination)
- 2 tablespoons of lemon juice (optional, to prevent browning)
- Sweetener (optional, to taste; you can use honey, maple syrup, or sugar)
- Additional flavorings (optional, such as cinnamon, vanilla extract, or grated ginger)

Instructions:

1. Preheat your oven to the lowest setting, typically around 140°F to 170°F (60°C to 75°C). If your oven doesn't go this low, use the lowest setting available.
2. Line a baking sheet with parchment paper or a silicone baking mat. Make sure the parchment paper or mat extends slightly beyond the edges of the baking sheet to prevent the fruit puree from dripping onto the pan.
3. In a blender or food processor, puree the chopped fruit until smooth. If using lemon juice, add it to the blender along with the fruit. If desired, add sweetener and any additional flavorings to the blender and blend until well combined.
4. Pour the fruit puree onto the prepared baking sheet, spreading it evenly into a thin layer with a spatula. Make sure the puree is spread evenly to ensure even drying.
5. Place the baking sheet in the preheated oven and bake the fruit puree for 4 to 6 hours, or until the fruit leather is dry to the touch and no longer sticky.
6. Once the fruit leather is dry, remove it from the oven and let it cool completely on the baking sheet.
7. Once cooled, use scissors or a sharp knife to cut the fruit leather into strips or squares. Roll each strip or square tightly and store them in an airtight container at room temperature for up to a week.
8. Enjoy your homemade fruit leather as a healthy and delicious snack!

You can customize your DIY fruit leather by using different combinations of fruits and flavorings. Experiment with your favorite fruits and get creative with different flavor combinations to find your perfect recipe. Enjoy!

Caprese Skewers (tomato, mozzarella, and basil)

Ingredients:

- Cherry tomatoes
- Fresh mozzarella balls (bocconcini or ciliegine)
- Fresh basil leaves
- Balsamic glaze or balsamic reduction (optional)
- Wooden skewers

Instructions:

1. Wash the cherry tomatoes and basil leaves. Drain the mozzarella balls if they're packed in liquid.
2. Thread one cherry tomato onto a wooden skewer, followed by a mozzarella ball and a basil leaf. Repeat the pattern until the skewer is filled, leaving a little space at each end for easy handling.
3. Arrange the assembled Caprese skewers on a serving platter.
4. Optional: Drizzle the assembled skewers with balsamic glaze or balsamic reduction for added flavor and presentation.
5. Serve the Caprese skewers immediately as an elegant appetizer or hors d'oeuvre.

These Caprese skewers are simple to assemble, yet they're bursting with fresh flavors. They're perfect for parties, gatherings, or as a light and refreshing snack. Enjoy!

Turkey and Veggie Stir-Fry

Ingredients:

- 1 pound turkey breast or turkey tenderloin, thinly sliced
- 2 tablespoons soy sauce
- 1 tablespoon oyster sauce
- 1 tablespoon sesame oil
- 2 cloves garlic, minced
- 1 inch ginger, minced
- 1 onion, thinly sliced
- 2 bell peppers, thinly sliced (any color you prefer)
- 1 cup broccoli florets
- 1 cup snow peas, trimmed
- Cooked rice or noodles, for serving

Instructions:

1. In a small bowl, mix together the soy sauce and oyster sauce. Set aside.
2. Heat the sesame oil in a large skillet or wok over medium-high heat. Add the minced garlic and ginger, and sauté for about 30 seconds until fragrant.
3. Add the thinly sliced turkey to the skillet and stir-fry for 3-4 minutes, or until cooked through.
4. Add the sliced onion, bell peppers, broccoli florets, and snow peas to the skillet. Stir-fry for an additional 4-5 minutes, or until the vegetables are tender-crisp.
5. Pour the soy sauce and oyster sauce mixture over the turkey and vegetables in the skillet. Stir to coat everything evenly and cook for another minute or two until heated through.
6. Taste and adjust seasoning if necessary. You can add more soy sauce or oyster sauce if desired.
7. Remove the skillet from heat and serve the turkey and veggie stir-fry hot over cooked rice or noodles.
8. Garnish with sliced green onions or sesame seeds, if desired.

This turkey and veggie stir-fry is versatile, so feel free to customize it with your favorite vegetables or add extra ingredients like mushrooms, carrots, or snap peas. It's a delicious and satisfying meal that's perfect for a quick weeknight dinner. Enjoy!

Veggie Pita Pizzas

Ingredients:

- Whole wheat pita bread rounds
- Pizza sauce or marinara sauce
- Shredded mozzarella cheese
- Assorted vegetables (such as bell peppers, onions, mushrooms, tomatoes, spinach, olives, etc.), chopped or sliced
- Olive oil
- Italian seasoning or dried oregano (optional)
- Red pepper flakes (optional)

Instructions:

1. Preheat your oven to 375°F (190°C).
2. Place the pita bread rounds on a baking sheet lined with parchment paper or aluminum foil.
3. Spread a thin layer of pizza sauce or marinara sauce over each pita bread round, leaving a small border around the edges.
4. Sprinkle shredded mozzarella cheese evenly over the sauce on each pita bread round.
5. Top the pizzas with your choice of assorted vegetables. Be creative and use a variety of colors and flavors.
6. Drizzle a little olive oil over the top of each pizza for added flavor and to help the vegetables roast nicely.
7. If desired, sprinkle Italian seasoning or dried oregano over the pizzas for extra flavor. You can also add a pinch of red pepper flakes for a bit of heat.
8. Place the baking sheet in the preheated oven and bake the veggie pita pizzas for 10-12 minutes, or until the cheese is melted and bubbly and the edges of the pitas are golden brown.
9. Remove the pizzas from the oven and let them cool for a minute or two before slicing.
10. Slice the veggie pita pizzas into wedges or squares and serve hot.

These veggie pita pizzas are versatile, customizable, and perfect for using up leftover vegetables. They're a healthier alternative to traditional pizza and can be enjoyed as a meal or a snack. Feel free to experiment with different toppings and flavor combinations to suit your taste preferences. Enjoy!

Banana Oatmeal Cookies

Ingredients:

- 2 ripe bananas, mashed
- 1 cup old-fashioned oats
- 1/4 cup raisins or chocolate chips (optional)
- 1/4 cup chopped nuts (such as walnuts or pecans) (optional)
- 1/2 teaspoon ground cinnamon (optional)
- 1/4 teaspoon vanilla extract (optional)

Instructions:

1. Preheat your oven to 350°F (175°C). Line a baking sheet with parchment paper or lightly grease it with cooking spray.
2. In a mixing bowl, mash the ripe bananas with a fork until smooth.
3. Add the old-fashioned oats to the mashed bananas and stir until well combined. If using, add the raisins or chocolate chips, chopped nuts, ground cinnamon, and vanilla extract to the mixture and stir until evenly distributed.
4. Using a spoon or cookie scoop, drop spoonfuls of the banana oatmeal cookie dough onto the prepared baking sheet, spacing them about 2 inches apart.
5. Flatten each cookie slightly with the back of a spoon or your fingers, as they won't spread much during baking.
6. Bake the banana oatmeal cookies in the preheated oven for 12-15 minutes, or until they are golden brown around the edges.
7. Remove the cookies from the oven and let them cool on the baking sheet for a few minutes before transferring them to a wire rack to cool completely.
8. Once cooled, store the banana oatmeal cookies in an airtight container at room temperature for up to 3-4 days.

These banana oatmeal cookies are soft, chewy, and naturally sweetened by the ripe bananas. They're perfect for a quick and nutritious snack, breakfast on-the-go, or a guilt-free dessert option. Enjoy!

Mini Tacos

Ingredients:

- Mini taco shells or tortilla cups
- Ground beef or turkey
- Taco seasoning
- Shredded lettuce
- Diced tomatoes
- Shredded cheese (such as cheddar or Mexican blend)
- Sour cream
- Guacamole or diced avocado
- Salsa

Instructions:

1. Preheat your oven to 350°F (175°C). Place the mini taco shells or tortilla cups on a baking sheet and warm them in the oven according to the package instructions, typically for 3-5 minutes.
2. In a skillet over medium heat, cook the ground beef or turkey until it's browned and cooked through, breaking it apart with a spoon as it cooks.
3. Drain any excess grease from the cooked meat and stir in the taco seasoning according to the package instructions. Cook for an additional minute to allow the flavors to meld.
4. Fill each mini taco shell or tortilla cup with a spoonful of the cooked meat mixture.
5. Top the mini tacos with shredded lettuce, diced tomatoes, shredded cheese, sour cream, guacamole or diced avocado, and salsa, as desired.
6. Serve the mini tacos immediately as a delicious appetizer or snack.

These mini tacos are customizable, so feel free to add your favorite taco toppings such as black beans, corn, diced onions, cilantro, or jalapeños. They're sure to be a hit with guests of all ages! Enjoy!

Ham and Cheese Pinwheels

Ingredients:

- 1 sheet puff pastry, thawed
- Dijon mustard (optional)
- Thinly sliced ham
- Sliced cheese (such as Swiss or cheddar)
- Egg wash (1 egg beaten with 1 tablespoon water)

Instructions:

1. Preheat your oven to 400°F (200°C). Line a baking sheet with parchment paper or lightly grease it with cooking spray.
2. Roll out the thawed puff pastry sheet on a lightly floured surface into a rectangle, about 1/4 inch thick.
3. If using, spread a thin layer of Dijon mustard evenly over the puff pastry sheet.
4. Layer the thinly sliced ham over the puff pastry sheet, covering the entire surface.
5. Place the sliced cheese on top of the ham, overlapping slightly if needed.
6. Starting from one long edge, tightly roll up the puff pastry sheet into a log, like a jelly roll.
7. Once rolled, use a sharp knife to slice the log into 1/2-inch thick pinwheels.
8. Place the pinwheels cut-side down on the prepared baking sheet, spacing them a few inches apart.
9. Brush the tops of the pinwheels with the egg wash, which will help them turn golden brown as they bake.
10. Bake the ham and cheese pinwheels in the preheated oven for 12-15 minutes, or until they are puffed up and golden brown.
11. Remove the pinwheels from the oven and let them cool slightly on the baking sheet before serving.
12. Serve the ham and cheese pinwheels warm as a delicious appetizer or snack.

These ham and cheese pinwheels are sure to be a hit at parties, gatherings, or any time you're craving a savory treat. Feel free to customize them with your favorite cheeses, meats, or additional fillings. Enjoy!

Sweet Potato Toast with Toppings

Ingredients:

- 1 large sweet potato
- Toppings of your choice (see suggestions below)

Instructions:

1. Wash and scrub the sweet potato thoroughly to remove any dirt. Pat it dry with a paper towel.
2. Slice the sweet potato lengthwise into 1/4-inch thick slices. You can use a sharp knife or a mandoline slicer for even slices.
3. Toast the sweet potato slices in a toaster or toaster oven until they are tender and cooked through. This may take 2-3 cycles in the toaster, depending on the thickness of the slices.
4. Once the sweet potato slices are toasted, remove them from the toaster and let them cool slightly before adding toppings.
5. Here are some delicious topping ideas for sweet potato toast:
    - Avocado slices and a sprinkle of red pepper flakes
    - Almond butter or peanut butter with sliced bananas and a drizzle of honey
    - Hummus with sliced cucumber, cherry tomatoes, and fresh herbs
    - Ricotta cheese with sliced strawberries and a drizzle of balsamic glaze
    - Cream cheese with smoked salmon, capers, and fresh dill
    - Greek yogurt with mixed berries and a sprinkle of granola
    - Mashed avocado with sliced hard-boiled eggs and Everything Bagel seasoning
    - Pesto sauce with roasted cherry tomatoes and fresh basil leaves
    - Sautéed spinach and mushrooms with a fried or poached egg on top
6. Arrange the toppings of your choice on the sweet potato toast slices and serve immediately.

Sweet potato toast with toppings is a delicious and satisfying breakfast, snack, or light meal option that's packed with flavor and nutrients. Get creative with your favorite toppings and enjoy!

Cucumber Sandwiches

Ingredients:

- Bread slices (white, whole wheat, or your favorite variety)
- Cream cheese or softened butter
- English cucumber, thinly sliced
- Fresh dill or chives, chopped (optional)
- Salt and pepper to taste

Instructions:

1. Trim the crusts off the bread slices, if desired. This step is optional, but it gives the cucumber sandwiches a more elegant appearance.
2. Spread a thin layer of cream cheese or softened butter evenly over each bread slice. Make sure to spread all the way to the edges to prevent the sandwiches from getting soggy.
3. Arrange the thinly sliced cucumber rounds evenly over half of the bread slices, covering them completely.
4. If using, sprinkle chopped fresh dill or chives over the cucumber slices for added flavor.
5. Season the cucumber slices with a pinch of salt and pepper to taste. Be careful not to oversalt, as the cream cheese or butter already adds some saltiness.
6. Place the remaining bread slices on top of the cucumber slices to form sandwiches. Press down gently to adhere the layers together.
7. Using a sharp knife, carefully cut each sandwich into quarters or halves, depending on your preference.
8. Serve the cucumber sandwiches immediately as a delightful and refreshing appetizer or snack.

Cucumber sandwiches are best enjoyed fresh, as the cucumber slices can release moisture and make the bread soggy if left for too long. However, you can prepare the components ahead of time and assemble the sandwiches just before serving to save time. Enjoy these light and tasty treats!

DIY Fruit Cups

Ingredients:

- Assorted fresh fruits (such as strawberries, blueberries, raspberries, blackberries, grapes, pineapple, melon, kiwi, etc.)
- Small plastic cups or containers with lids
- Lemon juice (optional, to prevent browning)
- Honey or agave syrup (optional, for added sweetness)

Instructions:

1. Wash and dry the fresh fruits thoroughly. If using fruits that brown easily (such as apples or bananas), you can toss them in lemon juice to prevent browning.
2. Chop the fruits into bite-sized pieces. Try to cut them into uniform sizes for a more visually appealing presentation.
3. Layer the chopped fruits into the small plastic cups or containers, alternating colors and textures to create a visually appealing display.
4. If desired, drizzle a little honey or agave syrup over the layered fruits for added sweetness. You can also sprinkle some lemon zest or fresh mint leaves for extra flavor.
5. Once the fruit cups are assembled, cover them with lids and store them in the refrigerator until ready to serve.
6. Serve the DIY fruit cups chilled as a refreshing snack or light dessert. They're perfect for picnics, lunchboxes, or any time you're craving something sweet and nutritious.

These DIY fruit cups are customizable, so feel free to use your favorite fruits or whatever is in season. You can also add yogurt, granola, or nuts for extra protein and texture.

Enjoy these delicious and healthy treats!

Cheesy Cauliflower Bites

Ingredients:

- 1 head of cauliflower, cut into florets
- 1 cup shredded cheddar cheese
- 1/4 cup grated Parmesan cheese
- 1/4 cup breadcrumbs
- 1 teaspoon garlic powder
- 1/2 teaspoon paprika
- Salt and pepper to taste
- 2 eggs, beaten
- Cooking spray or olive oil

Instructions:

1. Preheat your oven to 400°F (200°C). Line a baking sheet with parchment paper or lightly grease it with cooking spray or olive oil.
2. Steam the cauliflower florets until they are tender but still firm, about 5-7 minutes. Drain well and let them cool slightly.
3. In a large mixing bowl, combine the steamed cauliflower florets, shredded cheddar cheese, grated Parmesan cheese, breadcrumbs, garlic powder, paprika, salt, and pepper. Mix until well combined.
4. Add the beaten eggs to the cauliflower mixture and stir until everything is evenly coated.
5. Using your hands or a spoon, shape the cauliflower mixture into small bite-sized balls or patties and place them on the prepared baking sheet.
6. Lightly spray the cauliflower bites with cooking spray or drizzle them with a little olive oil for added crispiness.
7. Bake the cheesy cauliflower bites in the preheated oven for 20-25 minutes, or until they are golden brown and crispy on the outside.
8. Remove the cauliflower bites from the oven and let them cool slightly before serving.
9. Serve the cheesy cauliflower bites warm as a delicious snack or appetizer. You can enjoy them on their own or dip them in your favorite sauce, such as marinara sauce, ranch dressing, or tzatziki.

These cheesy cauliflower bites are sure to be a hit with both kids and adults. They're a great way to sneak some extra veggies into your diet while enjoying a cheesy and satisfying snack. Enjoy!